FC POEMS

LUCY MATTHEWS did the pics.
ALAN HAYWARD wrote the verse.

Why not **LUCY'S** poems? No!
ALAN'S pictures? Even worse!

For Kim

Alan Hayward

Printed in Great Britain

Summersdale Publishers
46 West Street
Chichester
West Sussex
PO19 1RP
United Kingdom

A CIP catalogue record for this book is available from the British Library.

ISBN 1 84024 045 8

About the Author and the Illustrator

Alan Hayward is a retired physicist who spent his working life doing scientific research. He has patented numerous inventions and published eight non-fiction books.

Retirement has given him the chance to spend more time on the things he enjoys most. One of them is writing comic verses to amuse children, and *Fun-Poems* contains a selection of these. He lives at Portishead in Somerset.

Lucy Matthews has for many years been an illustrator of children's literature. She spent ten years working for the Daily Express, illustrating the adventures of Rupert Bear.

More recently she has made a name for herself as a Cornish landscape artist. She lives and has her studio near Penzance.

Contents

Beeline

A happy little butterfly
Zigzagged her way across the sky.
She met a bee, who said, "How do!
I fly straight lines, so why can't you?"

She said, "I'd rather stay like me,
For you're a workaholic bee.
Don't work your fingers to the bone;
Be wise, enjoy life, be a drone!"*

* A drone is a kind of bee who never works. His only duty is to go to bed with the queen bee.

You Can't Teach an Old Cow New Tricks

Pat-a-cake, pat-a-cake, farmer's man,
Make me a dung-heap as fast as you can.
Prick it and pat it and bang it down hard,
And don't go and drop bits all over the yard.

   "Farmer, Sir, Farmer, Sir, please may I ask:
   Can't we abolish this smelly old task?
   Babies use potties, Puss digs little holes;
   Why can't our cattle drop theirs into bowls?"

Don't talk such nonsense, my dear farmer's man.
How can a cow learn to sit on a pan?
Don't waste your time by inventing a loo
For cows, who would only protest, "Moo, moo,
   MOO!"

Real Nuts

Tom Squirrel went to market
To buy a bag of nuts.
He picked a huge, great big one,
For he's a greedy guts.

But when he tried to lift it,
It weighed an awful lot.
He frowned, and asked, "Are these things
Giant coconuts, or what?"

The shopman grinned, and told him,
"You shouldn't come to me.
My nuts are brass and steel ones.
They go on bolts, you see."

Who's Afraid of Mary?

Mary, Mary, quite contrary,
How does your lifestyle go?
"With magic spells, and bells and smells,
And broomsticks all in a row!"

Mary, Mary, you're no fairy.
You cut no ice with me.
You're not a witch; you're growing rich
Through bluff and trickery.

I know your curse will be no worse
Than water on a goose.
Why should I fear you, Mary dear,
Your magic is no use!

You make me laugh. You're just not half
The witch you claim to be.
You can't whisk me across the sea,
You have no power to ....
.....................wheeeeeeeee!

[Hey, what's happened? He's disappeared!]

Hippo in a Hole

A fat old, happy hippo
Went out to take a stroll.
Bad luck! For that old hippo
Fell down a great big hole.

But Hippy wasn't worried.
He said, "Back in the zoo
Where I'm a star attraction,
They'll know just what to do.

"They'll send men out to find me,
And when they see I'm here,
They'll get a crane to lift me,
And free me, never fear."

Poor Hippy was mistaken.
They sent a crane, all right,
But found it couldn't lift him,
For he was wedged, quite tight.

His keepers, full of patience,
Then tried another way:
They filled the hole with water.
(It took them half a day.)

Old Hipp thought that was lovely.
He wallowed in the goo,
And with a stylish breast-stroke
Swam right back to the zoo.

The Guzzler

Mr. Guzzledy-Gulpity-Gobbly McGhee
(Known as Mac) has a craving to drink cups of tea.
He'll drink ten in the morning, ten more before bed,
And another ten cups in the night, I've heard said.

In his youth he was normal, then something went wrong.
When in hospital, Mac (who had stayed there too long)
Had a tired little nurse who made such a bad slip
That she plugged in a flask of cold tea to his drip.

When she saw what she'd done, she cried out, "Oh,
    dear me!
Oh, that poor man's transfusion's not blood, it is tea!"
Then she screamed, "Doctor, Doctor!" - an earsplitting
    shout.
But he said, "You're too late, for I can't take it out."

Thus, the tea that went into Mac's veins on that day
Is there still, for it clings and it won't go away.
So old Guzzledy Mac has got tea in his blood,
Which explains why he drinks such an unending flood.

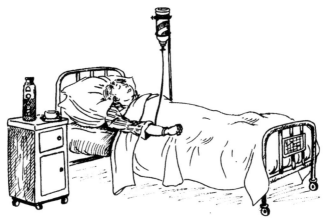

I Believe

There IS a Loch Ness Monster,
Yes, deep down in the water,

At times when no one's watching
She'll part the water surface,
pluck up all her courage,
And when she's really daring,
She'll

in Nessie

I know that she exists.
she lurks all turns and twists.
and shove a great loop
she'll briefly come in view.
through.
OUT!!
knot
she'll leave no room for doubt:
and poke her top

Monkey Tricks

A monastery garden
Was overrun by skunks,
And, though they're kindly people,
This didn't please the monks.

The monastery father
Said, "Brothers, let us pray
That all these horrid creatures
Will up, and run away."

The skunks felt quite insulted.
They said, "Now let us spray,
And teach these monkish fellows
That we can win the day."

A hundred tails were lifted,
And every one went: SQUIRT!
The smell was quite appalling -
Much worse than getting hurt.

The youngest monk spoke slowly.
"My brothers - look - perhaps
We ought to get some gasmasks,
Then catch the skunks in traps?"

The head monk said, "Too cruel!
Now this is what I say.
We'll soak ourselves in perfume,
And chase the skunks away."

They did so, using rose-oil,
A lovely-smelling scent.
And when the skunks first smelled it,
They panicked - and they went!

For just as we hate skunk-stink,
Skunks hate a smell that's good.
(You know what drives them crazy?
The smell of Christmas Pud!)

Tortoise Won? Don't be Daft!

Hare and Tortoise had a race.
Hare-kept-up-a-spanking-pace.
While . . the . . poor . . old . . stiff . . tortoise . . just . .
  . . plodded . . along,
As . . he . . whistled . . the . .Dead. . March . . by . . way . .
  . . of . . a . . song.

Hare-glanced-back-and-gave-a-grin,
"Poor-old-Tortoise-you-can't-win!"
But . . persistent . . old . . Tortoise . . just . . kept . .
  . . on . . and . . on,
Until . . Hare . . had . . long . . finished . . the . . course . .
  . . and . . had . . gone.

Those nuts who tell kids Tortoise won,
Don't realise how much harm they've done.
The fact is, Hare is always first,
While poor old Tortoise comes off worst.

Most times, the hares grow rich and fat,
While tortoises get none of that.
In marriage - wow! - you can't compare 'em,
For tortoises can't have a harem!*

* *The word "harem" doesn't really have anything to do with hares.*
 Some rich men in Asia have a whole lot of wives, and they call this collection of wives their harem. It is an Arabic word, meaning, "Hands off, you guys!"

Elephants are Great

An elephant never forgets, so it's said.
He stores it all up in his clever old head.
He knows mathematics, and how to prune trees,
And how to make centipedes bend all their knees.

He knows the best ways to have masses of fun,
And the number of miles from the earth to the
    sun.
He knows all the kings back to William the Conk,
And the way to reply when a goose says, "Honk,
    honk!"

An elephant *never* forgets, do you hear?
He hangs on to all that goes in his big ear.
Just take it from me that this really is so -
I happen to be one myself, so I know.

Because I'm a jumbo, I never forget -
I've never forgotten a single thing yet.
My elephant memory's awfully strong,
My elephant memory never goes wrong.

My poem runs on, with an elegant grace,
Extolling the worth of our elephant race.
So shall I continue? Er . . no . . perhaps not
Oh, dear . . the fact is . . I've forgotten the lot . .

Modern Miss Muffet

Modern Miss Muffet
Sat on a tuffet,
  Eating her spicy fish stew.
There came a black spider,
And sat down beside her.
  Miss Modern knew just what to do.
 She snatched up a fly-swat
And walloped old Black Spot
- then dropped his remains in the stew.
                    Phew!

The Hungry Tiger

The old caveman stood silent, his eyes open wide.
In his cave there was nowhere to run, or to hide.

At the mouth of the cave, he could see a great
    Shape
Which was hunting for dinner; he couldn't escape!

That great Shape was a sabre-toothed tiger, no
    less,
So the caveman could see no way out of this mess.

For he knew the beast's favourite dish was a man.
(It will also eat women, whenever it can,
But it never eats children, because they're too
    small
To fill its great tummy - they're no use at all.)

His poor heart nearly stopped, and he shook at
    the knees,
While his nose started tickling. He gave a great
    sneeze.

Then the sabre-tooth slammed on its brakes and
    stopped dead.
"I might catch that man's cold and be ill!" the
    beast said.
"I must look somewhere else for my next joint of
    meat,
For this germ-laden man is just not fit to eat."

"Hip-hooray!" said the man. "I'll feel safe, every
    day,
Now I know that loud sneezing keeps tigers away."

The Llama is No Charmer

I thought I'd like a lama
For Christmas, as a pet.
So good old Santa brought one.
(He got it from the vet.)

But he's a problem llama.
I don't know what to do.
I couldn't have more headaches
If Santa'd brought a zoo.

I don't know how to spell him -
With one L, two, or three?
I don't know how to feed him -
What should he have for tea?

He's quite a little lllama,
His legs aren't very thick.
His hooves are rather tiny,
But, wow! He can't half kick.

I'd thought that I could ride him,
But that's not his idea.
I wouldn't dare to mount him;
No way! Not me! No fear!

He has a nasty custom
That I don't like a bit.
When he gets really angry
He'll look your way and spit.
And sometimes it will miss you;
But sometimes it will hit.

Educating the Old Mother

Old Mother Hubbard
Went to the cupboard
To get her poor doggy a bone.
But her spoilt little pet
Glared and said, all upset,
"I hate those old dry things, groan, groan!

"Such grub's out of date.
How long must I wait
For you to catch up with the news?
Have you not heard of tins
Full of doggy din-dins?
Just let me come shopping, and choose!"

Whodunnit

I was cruising around in the squad car
When the voice on the radio said,
"Crematorium! Quick! You must stop him,
Or a live bloke will soon join the dead!"

So we screeched to a halt in the car park
By the sign, SPACE RESERVED FOR THE
   HEARSE,
While the lady in charge rushed to meet us,
With a face like a corpse's - or worse.

When we asked her just what was the trouble,
She was trembling. She whispered, "Don't know.
There's a man up on top of the steeple.
Least, there *was*. He looked perched on one toe.

"He was first seen on top of the chimney,
And from there he jumped up to the spire.
While I phoned for assistance, he vanished.
Where's he now? That's for you to enquire."

Then we looked all around; no dead body
Or injured man lay on the ground.
Both her colleagues told much the same story,
So it seemed that her mind was quite sound.

I then asked, "Can you give a description?
Could you see the man's face from below?"
She went whiter than ever, and muttered,
"He's the double of someone I know;

"Of a man we cremated this morning,
A peculiar guy, a near-freak.
I keep seeing his face in my mind, still.
What a nose! Long and sharp, like a beak.

"When he came in to see me last Friday
He was on his last legs, a real wreck.
He explained that he'd soon want cremation,
And he paid in advance with a cheque.

"Then he promptly collapsed, and the doctor
That I summoned arrived just too late.
So the police did their usual post-mortem
And then gave us the corpse to cremate.

"His identity still is a riddle,
As is that of his look-alike, too.
Take a look at his cheque, would you, Sergeant.
It's signed 'Phoenix'.*   Could that be a clue?"

*If you don't know what a phoenix is, you'd find it
interesting to look it up in a dictionary.

Golfin' Dolphin

I once met a dolphin who said he liked golfing,
And he asked me to play a few holes.
I asked, "Why not cricket?" He said, "I can't stick
  it!
I'm so scared of that strong bloke who bowls.

"I like to play slow games, not get-up-and-go
  games.
That's why golf is the sport I like best."
So I had to agree, and we moved to the tee,
Though I thought him a bit of a pest.

So's to get there, he slid on his tail (yes, he did!)
Holding head and beak high in the air.
With his club in his mouth, he teed off towards
  south,
And his ball flew, but no one knew where.

So we walked to first hole, and we pulled out the
  pole,
While old Dolph seemed to think it was fun.
And he wasn't surprised when spectators advised,
"There's your ball! It's a real hole-in-one!"

I could hardly play on, for my strength was all
  gone,
And I thought I was playing in vain.
But I need not have feared, and I soon was much
  cheered,
For he never once did it again.

At the close of our play, I decided to pay
For a beer for my new golfing pal.
As we drank, I said, "Now, will you tell me just
  how
You could play that first hole so darned well?"

He then gave a broad grin, and he waggled a fin.
"You see, dolphins have friends by the shoal.
I've a squirrel on call, and he picked up my ball,
And he carted it off to the hole!"

Guess What I Am

What a life! There is no one who loves me, not
  one;
There is no one who wants me to have any fun.
There's just one thing I'm good at, and when I do
  that,
They will moan, or they'll tremble, or squawk like
  a cat.

I am sure that they'd like me to curl up and die.
When I think of their hatred, I break down and
  cry.
They've attempted to murder me, time after time;
Yes, they're villains, they're devils, they're hardened
  in crime.

Ah, I know what you're thinking, you think I've
  gone mad,
To conclude the entire human race is so bad.
But they *are*. They keep trying to poison my
  meals.
As for you, you don't know how a poor victim
  feels.

And you'd hate me yourself, Sir, if only you knew
Just what kind of a creature I am, Sir, boo-hoo.
Now, excuse me, I'm growing quite weary . . ah . . er.
Oh, please, pity us poor old bacteria, Sir!

Kangaroo Fashions

Most kangaroos
Will just refuse
To wear smart shoes.
Instead, they choose
Long hairy trews.*
This garment goes
From hip to toes.
It's snug. Besides,
It also hides
From me and you
The ugly view
Of whopping feet,
Which don't smell sweet,
And don't look neat,
But fill the street.

* *A Scottish word for trousers.*

Counter-Attack

Old Robin Corke, a farming man,
Loved getting food for free.
There's nothing he enjoyed so much
As birds, deep-fried, for tea.

Each day he'd pull his wellies on
And stomp around his farm,
A hungry look upon his face,
A gun beneath his arm.

Each time he saw some poor old bird,
He'd stop and take a shot.
It never took him long to bag
Enough to fill his pot.

One day a flock of rooks said, "This
Must stop. We must attack.
We'll all swoop down at once, and then
Old Robin's nerve will crack."

Like fighter planes, they dived at him,
And took away his breath.
Indeed, it would be fair to say
They scared the bloke to death.

They made him lose his self-control,
And, in a panic, run.
And so he came to shoot himself,
By falling on his gun.

A tragic end. Poor Robin Corke;
A lonely death he died.
For none were sad and none did mourn;
He had no friends that cried.

All the birds of the air never fell a-sighing, sobbing,
When they heard of the death of poor Corke (Robin).
Instead, they started dancing and rejoicing, full of
    glee.
"Good riddance!" was the message that rang out
    from tree to tree.
Not a bird of the air even thought of sighing,
    sobbing,
When he heard of the death of poor Corke (Robin).

Air Traffic Control

King Puffin asked the seagulls,
"Why do you fly in Vees?"
The seagulls screeched and answered,
"We like it, if you please!"

King Puffin frowned, and grumbled,
"All very well for you!
You take up so much airspace
At times I can't get through."

The seagulls said, "Oh, sorry.
We don't mean any harm.
We'll break up into couples
And fly off arm-in-arm."

Jumbo Learns a Lesson

An elephant out walking
Once found a can of beer.
He picked it up and drank it.
He said, "It does taste queer.

"And yet I don't dislike it.
Why, there's another can!
I do believe a boxful
Has fallen off a van."

So Jumbo had another,
A third, a fourth, and more;
And soon the box was empty -
He'd drunk all twenty-four!

He gave a mighty hiccup,
And sat upon the floor.
He said, "I do feel funny;
There's something wrong, I'm sure."

He stood up straight - or tried to.
But, no, it wouldn't work.
His legs collapsed beneath him,
His trunk gave one last jerk.

He lay there, helpless, silent,
An elephantine heap.
He couldn't move a muscle,
He uttered not a cheep.

The passers-by ignored him.
They knew what he had done.
The empty cans around him
Showed how he'd had his fun.

It wasn't till next morning
That he at last came round,
And then it took him ages
To get up, off the ground.

He slowly staggered homewards.
He nursed his great, sick head.
He took a king-sized aspirin,
And clambered into bed.

He said, "Now I've discovered
That beer knocks jumbos flat.
Last night's will last a lifetime -
I want no more of that!"

But I Wanted a Camel!

A camel isn't cuddly.
That's what my Mummy said.
She wouldn't let me have one
To take upstairs to bed.

She says it's all humpaceous.
(I think that means it kicks.)
She says I couldn't ride it,
Because I'm only six.

She says the thing might bite me.
I don't see why it should,
'Cos camels aren't carnivlous.
(Hey, don't that word sound good!)

Oh, what's the use of talking?
My Mummy's mind's made up.
I guess I'll have to settle
For what she's bought - a pup.

The Disappearing Mermaid

There's a mermaid in our garden pond,
I'm sure there is, you know.
I've seen her bubbles rising up,
From round the rocks below.

There's a mermaid in our garden pond.
I've tried to tell my mum,
But she remarks, "Oh, really dear?"
And leaves me feeling glum.

There's a mermaid in our garden pond.
I've tried to tell my sister,
But she just scowls at me and says,
"Get lost, you little blister!"

There's a mermaid in our garden pond.
One day I went to see.
She brushed her long and flowing hair;
Blue eyes looked up at me.

There's a mermaid in our garden pond.
Do you know what she did?
She looked at me and blew a kiss,
And then she dived and hid.

by my granddaughter, Pippa Hayward (age 10)

*I've included this to show what young people can
achieve if they try hard enough.*
Now see what you can do!

FIREWORKS

I'm very fond of fireworks. There's Catherine wheels! They whizz and whoosh and spin. They're wizard though they make a din.

And then there's jumping crackers. When they jump, I jump too.

Some kids are scared of bangers.
But I'm not scared. Are you?

**My Dad will sometimes let me
Hold sparklers in my hand.**

**But holding other fireworks
Is absolutely banned**

You **NEVER** hold a rocket.
You mustn't even try.

For if you hold a rocket, you'll have to learn to fly!

I'M

TWO O'CLOCK

Oh, dear, I'm trapped without a

looked— I don't know what

follow me—You'll

Oh, dear, it looked as easy as it's not panic, kid, just "Don't

THREE O'CLOCK.

Caught.

RESCUER.

shout. FOUR O'CLOCK. It's

the name to Hampton

AMAZED

I'm in the maze at Hampton Court—I really think they

doubt,—I'm far inside

to do, I'm hooked—

still be home in

flipping ought—To change

no one hears me when I

my tea is cooked!

tea!

time for

Help! take me home!

and can't get out—And

Ah, Isn't he Wise

A daft old owl sat in an oak.
He said, "I'd like to crack a joke.
But that won't do (tu-whit tu-whoo!)
I look so sad, they'd think me mad."

This daft old owl sat in an ash.
He said, "I'd like to have a bash
At singing songs like Nightingale.
But that won't do - I'd only wail."

This daft old owl sat in a birch.
He said, "I'd like to go to church.
But then I'd have to pray, not prey.
So that won't do; I'll stop away."

This daft old owl sat in an elm.
He said, "I'd like to found a realm
Where birds are kings. But that won't do;
Big birds would reign, not me and you."

This daft old owl sat in a beech.
He said, "I'd like to try and reach
North Pole, for then I'd feel so bold.
But that won't do: I can't stand cold."

This daft old owl sat in a wood.
He said, "My thoughts are all no good.
To kid mankind that I am wise
I'll just sit still until I dies."

Help!

I find my hands don't reach the ceiling.
This gives me quite a worried feeling,
That, p'raps, one day, my feet, worse luck,
Won't reach the floor - and I'll be stuck!

Badger The Cadger

I knew a fat badger, a rotten old cadger,
Who'd beg for his food in the street.
He'd sit on a lounger, the terrible scrounger,
And hold out a tin with his feet.

A terrible boaster, he'd written a poster,
To say he deserved much support:
"I've a wife; she's a pet. And my kids? A full sett[+]
Our food? Just the little we've caught."

Without any wages, he sat there for ages,
That passers-by might give some food:
A beetle, a cat's paw, a worm, or a rat's jaw.
His tin stayed unfilled. He grew rude.

"You lot aren't half rotten! It seems you've forgotten,
We must have some food, or we'll die."
Up came a fierce vixen,[*] who carried a six-gun,
And this was her angry reply:

"We don't fancy giving, we work for our living!
I'll give you a lesson, not grub!
I'll grab you, and stab you, and cut you, and gut
    you,
And sell your stuffed skin in a pub!"

For fear he'd be eated, the badger retreated
Rushed home to his wife, in the rain.
"Oh, do hold me tight, dear. I've had such a fright,
    dear.
I'll never go begging again!

[+] *A sett is an underground den.*

[*] *A vixen is a female fox.*

Christmas Mix-Up

Dear Santa,

Know what I'd like?
A little bike!
        Love
            Tracy

P.S.
    Oh, what a shame!
Can't spell your
        name.

Dear Tracy,

Mix me up with Satan? Why, that's shocking!
<u>Santa</u> is the one who fills your stocking.
S-A-N-T-A, just you remember,
Otherwise, no present next December.
For this year, here's a bike, straight from my
                                    sack,
Mixed up (like you) with handlebars at back.

                    Love
                        Santa.

Prickly Pair

"Now the thing I can't stand", said the porcupine's
    mate,
 "Is the way you expect me to patiently wait
While you finish your meal, before Mate can begin.
And you don't leave me much - it's no wonder I'm
    thin.

"And it's not only food that I'm starved of, you know;
I am short of affection, you old so-and-so!
Why, the rabbit's buck hugs her at least once a day;
Do I ever get petted, or cuddled? No way!"

So he told her what happened in nineteen-oh-eight,
When a lovable porcupine cuddled his mate.
For they each pressed their spikes in the other one's
    heart;
Thus their cuddle was ended, soon after the start.

Their loud shrieks were soon heard, and the
    neighbours were good:
They sought help, and the police came as fast as
    they could.
But the cops weren't much use, and they seemed not
    to know
What to do if they stayed there, or if they should go.

For the flabby old sergeant just scratched his thick
    head,
While the constable pulled out his notebook, and
    said,
"Cor, there's one of 'em dying, and one of 'em's dead,
And the floor is all stained such an 'orrible red."

Yes, they each stabbed the other to death (that's a
　fact).
It resembled (though wasn't) a suicide pact.*
What a tragedy! Oh! If we'd stopped them in time,
We'd have saved two young lives, two good porcs in
　their prime.

When the King of the Porcs heard the news, he was
　sad,
And he said, "That this happened is really too bad.
I must send out a law, throughout Porcupine Land:
PORCS MAY KISS IF THEY LIKE, BUT THE
　CUDDLE IS BANNED."

Old Smarty

I'm always a very smart leopard,
For I change all my spots every day.
I wear my socks once and then dump them.
I'm a beaut, not a brute, I may say.

I buy all my toppers from Harrods,
And my shoes are of crocodile skin.
I'm not like that scruffy old Tiger,
Whose torn pants are held up with a pin.

Just look at my exquisite shirt-front;
It's been starched, like my stiff upper lip.
While poor old, despicable Tiger
Wears the clothes that he finds on the tip.

If he should spend six months at charm school,
Why, he still couldn't knock spots off me -
And even if, somehow, he did so,
I could put them back on before tea!

Old Croc's Race

The crocodile's a funny shape,
Designed to see you can't escape.

His middle's thin, its length is great;

When chased by him,
His l$_e$ are short,
$_g$
$_s$

Then comes his tail, which guards his back.
With this bit, too, he can attack
His prey, because it's like a spear.
So keep away,
It's sharp.
Oh,
d
e
a
r
!

His jaws are savage as King Kong's
They'll grab you like a pair of tongs.

it's covered up by armour plate.

it isn't fun;
but can't h a run!
            l
          f

MISTER RAIN

When Rain falls straight

He never misses

He lands on me

like Gran's wet kisses

But when wind drives him to the side,

I know a nice dry place to hide.

"Then Rain runs off along the gutters and as he goes he sort of mutters, "I'll soon be diving down the drain." But I say, "Great! Good riddance, Rain!"

Poor Rain! The pipe he's in down there, is dark and smelly. He don't care!

He seems to know he'll soon get out
To join the river through the spout.

The river takes him to the sea,
And once he's there, Rain shouts "Whoopee!

"This place is home,
Sweet home, to me;
There's nowhere else
I'd rather be!"

But then the fierce hard=hearted Sun
Tells Water, "Now I'll spoil your fun!

I'll draw you up to share my sky,
Then you'll be clouds that float on high.

And that is real bad luck for me,
'Cos clouds won't stay there out at sea.
Comes whooshing down
On me again.
Then Mister Rain
They drift our way.

They Don't Want Me

When I went near the church, the priest chased me
away;
He just wouldn't accept that I'd come there to pray.
Why, if looks could have killed, I'd have dropped
down, stone dead,
And you'd never believe the rude things that he said.

Then he slammed the big door, with a great
thumping bang,
And I shivered, outside, while the choir inside sang,
"Oh-oh come, all ye faithful . . " The humbugs! The
beasts!
For they won't give a welcome to *me*, those dear
priests.

Yet I wouldn't give up. I came back, late at night.
I was wet, and dishevelled, and trembling with fright,
But I found what I wanted, without going far,
For the door to the vestry had been left ajar.

Once in there, it was easy to force my way in
To the chancel - the place where they preach against
sin.
Not that I am a sinner; of hell I've no fear,
For I did a good thing when I broke into here.

I've fulfilled my ambition, I've got what I want,
Now I'm close to the altar, the pulpit, and font.
For my Dad was a church-mouse, and Grandpa was,
too,
So I reckon it's fitting that I'm one, don't you?

Worm Power

There was a worm
Who owned a firm
Called "GARDENS DUG, DIRT CHEAP."
His workers crowned
Him King, and found
He promptly went to sleep.

Next day, with pride,
He woke and cried,
"Let's go and fight a war!
Take by surprise
And colonise
The field of slugs next door."

They said, "Agreed
If you will lead!"
And so King Worm went first.
The rest were slack;
They kept well back,
Because they feared the worst.

Their courage gone,
They slithered on.
At last they reached the bound
Of unknown land
Of rich, dark sand
Where treasures might be found.

King Worm yelled, "Now!
Let's make a vow
Of death or victory.
We shall not yield
Until this field
Belongs to you and me!"

But then King Worm
Began to squirm,
And in a panic cried,
"Look! Early Birds!
Oh, mark my words,
Each one of us must hide.

"Quick, down you go!
Down far below.
There's one thing you must learn.
We've not much power;
At such an hour,
Why, even worms must turn."

I DON'T LIKE ANTS

Ants

In your pants

Don't enhance

The pleasure you get from a picnic.

Run!

It's no fun

Being stung

So hide in the bushes and strip-quick.

The Leader

I am someone quite special, so listen with care.
I'm Augustus, T. H., and I'm great.
I belong to Class Four of Hill Junior School.
Teacher says that I'm really first-rate.

Yes, I'm way out in front of the rest of the class.
Not a boy or a girl can compare
With Augustus, T.H., for the way he behaves.
I don't grumble, play truant, or swear.

And I never tell lies, say rude things, or get cross.
Never once have I failed a class test.
So I think you'll agree that, without any doubt,
In Class Four I'm outstanding - the best.

All the others are jealous. You know what they
    call
Old Augustus, T. H.? "Teacher's pet!"
Oh, all right, they can say it, as much as they like,
Since it isn't a name to regret.

The fact is, I quite like it, I know that it's true.
Yes, it's just what I happen to be.
For I sit on her desk in my neat little cage.
I'm Augustus, The Hamster, that's me.

I Like Animals

White mice
Are nice.
So, of course,
Is the horse.
I adore
The wild boar,
And I love
The white dove.
But the lynx
Stynx.

A Serious Charge

The warthog told the rhino,
"We've got a chance of fame!
There is a competition
Especially for Big Game.

"It's like that old 'Miss World' one
But back to front, you see,
With prizes for the uglies -
For brutes like you and me."

The rhino grew indignant.
"You devil! To suggest
That I might come in your class
For looks! You little pest!"

The rhino put his head down,
And charged, just like a tank.
Then, when the warthog sidestepped,
He rammed a rocky bank.

His horn was bent and battered.
He cried, "I've hurt my head!"
"That's good. You quite deserved it",
The heartless warthog said.

"I'd take away your licence,
Were I a magistrate,
For speeding and not sounding
Your horn till far too late."

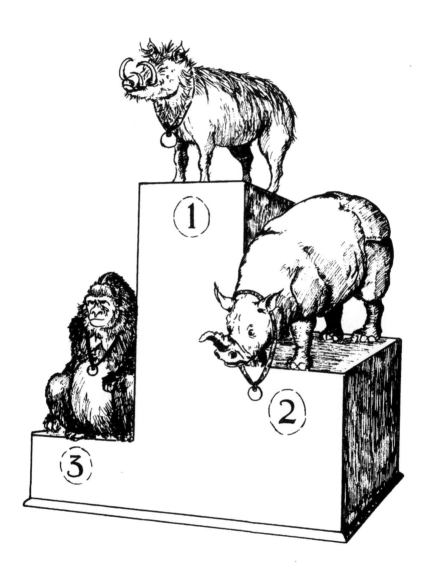

The Real Story
(But Don't Tell the Tiny Kids!)

Jack and Jill went up the hill,
To paint a water colour.
Jack loves things bright, like summer light;
Jill likes them rather duller.

They did no good; they never could
Agree on how to do it.
Jill said, "Today, do what I say!
What's that? You won't? I knew it!"

He turned and smiled. That made her wild.
She stamped and shook and shouted.
He wasn't cowed; he laughed out loud,
And that's how he got clouted.

She knocked him down, and broke his crown,
Then ran to fetch a doctor.
Jack lay in bed, with bandaged head,
And thought, "I wish I'd socked her!"

When Dinosaurs Disagreed

"Come off it!" screamed Diplodocus,
"Stop making this uncalled-for fuss.
Tyrannosaurus Rex is kind,
And you - you've got a nasty mind!

"T.Rex has been a friend to me.
I've been inside his den for tea,
And there I saw no sign of meat -
No skin, no bones, no tails, no feet.

"There's *no* proof he's a carnivore,
That's just a myth - just old wives' jaw.
All those who tell this wicked lie
Should blush with shame, until they die."

Just then, "Look out!" yelled Brontosaurus.
His words touched off a swelling chorus,
As every little dinosaurus
Cried, "Run! For we have life before us!"

But Dippy stood, with charming smile.
"Why, Mr. Rex! Please stay awhile.
I'll take you home to meet my Ma.
I'm sure she'll like you, and my ....Aaaaaarrgh!"

Oh, Doctor!

The surgery was over,
And I about to go,
When suddenly the phone rang.
I picked it up. "Hello?"

A voice said, "I need help, Doc.
I'm terrified of heights.
Can you prescribe some tablets
To set my mind to rights?"

I told her there was nothing
Which I could give for that.
She'd have to give up climbing,
And stay down on the flat;

To keep away from ladders,
And any open stair,
From cliffs, and tops of buses,
And not to go by air,

Since heights are not a peril
To those who stay down low.
She said, "You've got it wrong, Doc.
There's one thing you don't know.

"Your tips don't suit my case, Doc.
In fact, they make me laugh.
For I am not a girl, I'm
A twenty-foot giraffe!"

Irish Driving

An old train-driver, Pat, from Dun Laoghaire
      [If you try to pronounce it, be wary]
Said, "My job's become awfully scary.
    I daren't look at the track;
    So I'll sit at the back,
Saying, over and over, 'Hail, Mary!' "

Computer Games

6.....

I'm such a smart computer
That I can play good tricks.
So, though you've hit the nine-key,
I've put on screen a six.

6.....

Now don't you call me names, please,
I'm NOT a little swine!
Just stand upon your head, please,
And then you'll see your nine.

6.....

Hey, don't you dare to hit me,
You'll make my faceplate bend.
Just wait. I'll soon stop joking.
We'll get there in the end.

Mirrors are Cracked

A mirror is a funny thing,
For this is what I've found:
It makes the things that it reflects
Appear the wrong way round.

It's daft! It switches right and left,
And what I'd like to know
Is why it doesn't also put
Your top half down below?

THE BOUNCERS

Look, a bouncy castle!
No one on it, too!

That'll be for us, Joe.
Just for me and you.

Blow it. Here comes Charlie!
Don't let's let him stay.

Make him think we'll biff him,
Then he'll go away!

Author's note
Charlie's method is not recommended.

Heartbreak in the Haunted Hall

I'm a Thing that goes bump in the night.
Want a fright?

I can raise almost anyone's hair.
Want a scare?

I'm a ghastly old, bloodcurdling ghost.
That's my boast.

In old times, just one Wheeee! and they'd run.
Oh, what fun.

But today I'm successful no more.
What a bore.

These folk think that my act is a lie.
I could cry.

They just laugh when I rattle my chains.
Oh, it pains.

If I showed them my bones, they'd not care.
It's not fair.

Times is hard in the hall-haunting biz.
They sure is.

For the students I haunt don't believe.
How I grieve.

Halls of residence! Yuk! They are not
User-friendly for ghosts. Rotten lot!

The Octopus Ain't 'Armless

"I'm puzzled, Octopus. Look here!
Those wiggly things that look so queer,
That dangle down, all limp and loose -
Are they of any earthly use?

"They can't be legs, or every one
Would have a foot, so you could run.
They can't be arms, or each, I'm sure,
Would have a hand or else a claw."

The octopus replied, "Draw near
And I will whisper in your ear.
I'll show you what those things can do.
It's secret, though - just me and you!

"To start, I've wrapped them round your head,
And now I'll squeeze until you're dead!
So, though I have no hands or feet,
I'll feast today on nice fresh meat!"

Magic is Hard Work

A clueless old wizard once took a green lizard,
And turned the thing into (don't wince!)
A fat slug. He said, "Well! That's another dud spell;
This creature is really a prince.

"He was borrowed, you know, and I changed him,
    although
His mother said, 'Treat him with care.'
He has now been a cat, and a horse, and a bat,
A goat, and an old grizzly bear.

"Now, then, what's to do next? For the queen will be
    vexed,
If Princy walks home on four feet.
Why, it's me for the rack, if I can't turn him back
To Mummy's dear boy, Mummy's sweet.

"I shall try one last trick, but I'll have to be quick,
Or else he'll be late for his tea.
If he doesn't turn up, in good time for his cup
Of jelly (the royal kind) - poor me!"

With hands all a-tremble, he tried to assemble
A cauldron of sky-blue-pink fire.
But the stuff wouldn't light, and he thought, "Oh,
    good night!
I can't now escape the royal ire."

Then the slug crawled across. Slug was not at a loss;
He got the fire blazing, first try.
And it worked! He turned back to a prince, with the
    crack,
"So magic is now DIY!"

DRUMS ARE BEST

The brass trombone goes in and out,
while the sound of the horn goes
round about.

The fiddle-bow goes
In to's and fro's.

BUT THE DRUM!

WOW! THE DRUM!

YOU JUST WALLOP

AND IT MAKES SUCH A

THAT IT SHAKES THE WHOLE
ROOM!